I met you at dusk.
We loved till midnight.
Then, you left me.
2am found me at my lowest.
When the sun came up, I dried my tears,
found my strength,
and went on with my day.

2am Thoughts

MAKENZIE CAMPBELL

2018

Published by Central Avenue Publishing, an imprint of Central Avenue Marketing Ltd.
www.centralavenuepublishing.com

2AM THOUGHTS

Trade Paperback: 978-1-77168-164-3
Epub: 978-1-77168-165-0
Mobi: 978-1-77168-166-7

Published in Canada
Printed in United States of America

1. POETRY / General   2. POETRY / Love

19 18 17 16 15 14 13

To all who have believed, encouraged, and inspired me to write this.

Thank you.

You are holding my heart in your hands. My emotions have bled out on each and every page with the ink of my pen. Your eyes will discover my soul. Your fingers are casually flipping through my mind. I hope you find each delicate word as captivating as the stars. And I hope a piece of you feels what I felt when creating this art.

2am Thoughts

I'm so obsessed with falling in love that every time I meet a man, I lose myself in him.

3:59 PM

I like my rough edges. Smooth women are too easy to climb.

I don't like easy.

I want a man willing to hike mountains for me, or I don't want a man at all.

4:04 PM

My dream man does not consist of a perfectly structured face and well sculpted muscles. He, whoever he may be, does not have any physical requirements.

When I dream, I think of men who have the patience to wait hours for the wind while floating in the middle of the eternal sea. I think of caring and gentle eyes gazing into mine and giving me a sense of purpose. A heavy soul so deep and so complex it could take years to understand, but he never denies me a passageway into its thickness. An open heart that spills easily into mine, bleeding colors and painting memories.

I think of love. The ability he has to hold such a precious thing. The manner in which he carries such a fragile emotion. The way he is able to unconditionally love me for me.

4:08 PM

Life is to be lived—

To experience adventure.

To travel the world.

To learn exciting things.

And it is too short

to not.

4:11 PM

Do not let the dust collect in your soul.

Live a life so fulfilling that it will never have enough time to do so.

4:15 PM

My heart craves to feel a love that I have not encountered before. The kind that skips beats and summons butterflies.

4:17 PM

A BOY HAS NEVER LOVED ME

    although I wish one had.

So I keep waiting with all my emotions and all this love building inside me.

My heart waiting to thrive.

AND WHEN A BOY FINALLY DOES

Oh my, will my love be so deep for him. It might engrave beneath his bones.

4:18 P M

It had been forever since I had been in your arms. When you embraced me, even though a gesture as old friends, I fell right into you...

and fit perfectly.

4:31 PM

You are possibly the most beautiful and intricate human being I have ever met.

4:42 PM

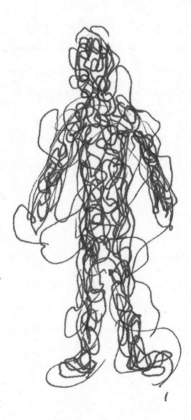

He is the type of person that has the entire night sky in his eyes. There are hurricanes and tornadoes underneath his skin. I swear every word, every breath, generates a windstorm. He holds the entire world in his heart.

I wish I could hold him in my arms.

4:45 PM

To spend a night with you would be marvelous.

Not for any physical pleasures. Do not get me wrong.

Rather to hear your aspirations and goals. What makes you cringe? What makes you smile? I want to know what your childhood was like. What were your troubles? What are your biggest fears? What do you dream about while you sleep? I want you to talk until the pattern of your voice vibrates my teeth and bones. I want to know every piece, every detail about you.

I want your heart. I want the rhythm of my heart to align with the drumming of yours.

I want you and I to not be you and I.

I want you and I to be us.

4:53 P M

They smelt strong. They smelt of rain and nature. Of pain and faith. Healing and sanction. They smelt like home.

His arms were my home.

5:00 PM

DUSK

Through all the darkness surrounding me, you somehow
found a way to shed light.

5:06 PM

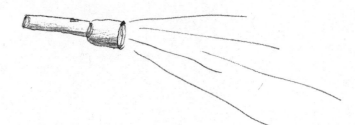

You call it love,

I'd say infatuation.

Now I am confused,

Is it you or me that is mistaken?

5:15 PM

Some songs seem to have people attached to them.

5:23 PM

Today I inked my skin with your name.

Not because I like the look and not because I love you. I got a tattoo because I like knowing it will never leave me even if you do.

5:49 PM

My lips are infused with the taste of you.

I just can't get enough.

6:01 PM

The way you spoke my name

        was enough to drive me insane.

The formation on your lips

        like a lettered kiss.

The euphonic melody

        was my drug, my remedy.

The song I play on repeat.

The one calming my tempestuous sea.

The only sound that sets me free.

                        6:19 PM

I need the contact, skin to skin, heart to heart, me to you.

I need the affection and attention you give me. No one looks at me the way you do. No one ever will.

7:00 P M

Maybe we are meant to be together. Maybe you are meant to tell me you love me.

Maybe when our worlds collided we were not meant to build our lives as separate people, but combine and build together.

7:02 PM

One day you too will have stopped searching strangers' eyes for companionship. You won't lie in a cold bed with nothing but dark thoughts to warm you. You will not order a pizza for yourself in your empty apartment.

One day you will have found your person. The one human being on this earth designed for you. The one that eases the pain in your heart and reminds you of why you are here. Why none of the other relationships worked. Why you had to go through heartache after heartache. And you will be thankful for all that pain because it now has brought so much happiness. You will look into your lover's eyes and feel something none of the others have made you feel. You will look into their eyes and realize they are the only ones you want to look into for the rest of your life.

You will no longer feel alone.

7:34 PM

You make me feel dangerous.

You dismiss the tiny voice in my head telling me to stop and nudge me to go.

You make me do things I never would have if I hadn't met you.

You make every day exciting,

thrilling,

electrifying.

You make me feel alive.

7:42 PM

Your eyes are precious gems.

I want to mine them

forever.

7:57 PM

I inhale your breath, your thoughts, your dreams.

And I refuse to exhale.

8:13 PM

You are a map of every destination I want to discover.

8:21 P M

My soul clings to yours. Each piece wedging into you, every vein tangling around your thoughts. Whole beats of my heart thumping your name.

I am hopelessly enthralled by your simple existence. The fact that somehow God could put together such a masterpiece of color and beauty.

You are a work of art.

8:48 PM

I'm into very messy love. Beautiful, crazy, messy love
spurred by our hearts.

8:51 PM

Your eyes are the sunrises and sunsets of my days.

8:56 P M

There was a time when I used to have panic attacks where I could barely breathe and hardly see. All I could think about was how no boy looked at me the way I wished. I would shake at the idea that I might never have anybody to love, nobody to tell my aspirations. I was so afraid that life would continue on like high school where I was overlooked and not interesting enough for a man to invest his time. These thoughts haunted me so often that I eventually believed I was simply unlovable.

But then you came along and when you realized I'm not what I thought men wanted me to be, you stayed. You never left my side. You kissed all the bruises and cuts my thoughts had scraped upon my heart. You healed my wounds entirely. You defeated my biggest fear. Now every time I look at you I remember that miserable young girl and how she was so completely wrong.

I am forever grateful for your love – the love that silenced my demons and calms the eternal storm taking place inside me.

9:11 PM

The love I have for you

burns faster than a forest fire.

9:18 PM

Feel the pitter-patter of the rain against your skin. Standing cold and alone in the slick streets under the light post.

Except you are not alone. I am beside you, falling into you, like the droplets that absorb into your pores. The water that slides down your cheeks and soaks your clothes, leaving you feeling heavier than before.

Feel the pitter-patter of my heart against your skin.

9:39 P M

You hold flecks of green in your grey eyes. Like emeralds burning, defying the darkness.

They are so immensely captivating.

I could get lost in them forever.

9:53 PM

I am not in control.

Love courses through my veins.

I cannot think straight.

I am the fastest car on Earth.

I have given my heart away to a ruthless boy.

Am I destined to crash and burn?

9:58 PM

Forever in a trance by your noncommittal romance.

10:13 PM

That's the problem: I am a tree and you are a leaf, easily swept away by the winds of someone better.

10:14 PM

Between my heart and my lips lies the filter of my thoughts.

10:18 PM

I build my own walls, yet I am

not strong enough to tear them down.

10:21 PM

When I'm with you I have all these words inside me ready to paint the world, but when they emerge, they are black and white because the colors get caught in my throat.

10:33 PM

Emotions are such a complex concept to understand.

10:34 PM

Do not hold my body.

Hold my heart.

Handle it with care.

For its faint drumming is fragile, unstable, and easily silenced.

Use the tender touch of your fingers to heal.

Remind me what a working heart beats like.

10:45 P M

The necessity to be desired eats away at us all.

10:50 PM

As the time ticks

down you start

to tick

away.

10:59 PM

All I've ever wanted is to feel wanted by you.

11:11 PM

A promise is the currency of love.

You can't afford to break it.

11:13 PM

I love the way you say my name and how your lips form.
But your tongue is weaponized with lies and now I'm torn
between wanting you and getting over you.

What the hell am I supposed to do?

11:14 PM

You paint me

suns and flowers

and beautiful landscapes

only to go back

and change them

to storms.

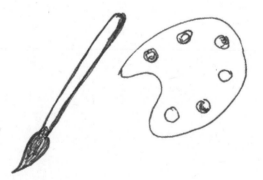

When you claimed you were working late and instead found yourself in another woman's bed in the dark, each body part melting into the next, and then regretted it the following morning, you told me it was a moment of weakness.

It wasn't.

It was a moment of truth.

11:25 P M

We create storms.

Brutal, beautiful storms.

So loud and bright they wake the neighbors.

But no one helps to calm them nor do they hide in safety.

They just stare, mesmerized by our show.

They cannot tell if it started with vexation or infatuation.

They cannot tell if we are falling in love or out of it.

11:29 PM

I had parts of the sky in my eyes and traces of the soil
beneath my fingers. The branches of evergreens climbing up
my back and tulips blooming in my soul.

But you weren't made for mountains and rivers and sunsets.
You were made for cities, skyscrapers, and starless nights.

I found that out the moment the grass growing between
your toes became an annoying itch.

11:30 PM

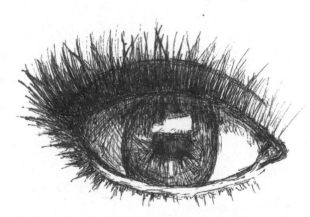

You say you want us to survive the flames, yet you feed the fire every time you walk away.

11:31 PM

Yes, you hear me.

But are you really listening?

11:34 PM

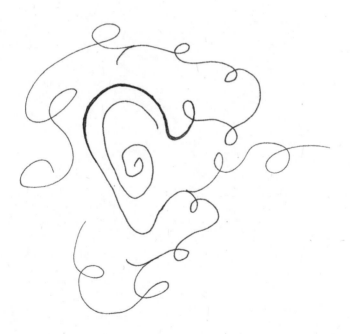

Those words both mended and broke my heart.

"I love you," he said.

Yet I still can't figure out how he could love me and leave me at the same time.

It's not over.

Not for you. Not for me.

We still relive each moment as we lay our heads
down to sleep.

But our faces remain as blank and empty as our hearts.
Or at least how we wish our hearts to be.

Right now, our love is blistering hot all over that organ.

We just excel in pretending.

11:45 P M

I tried to convince myself

      that one more night with you

           would change things.

over and over and over.

Until I had crumpled together in my hand one hundred
nights with you and still this empty feeling in my chest.

11:48 PM

Your touch has scarred my mind and clouded my memory.
Constantly thinking of you is tiring. Longing for you to
shelter my unwanted heart is unrealistic and hopeless. But
knowing all this, I seem to run back to you, and you, to me.

Why do our hearts make the same mistakes over and over?
Why do we always return only to leave again?

Why is it we come back when we know it's not right?

We think this time may be different, but it won't. I am the
shore and you are the tide. We come together only to get
pulled in opposite directions. And we repeat this cycle, over
and over. Yet as we continue to reach for one another, we
never accept the undeniable truth . . .

That no matter how hard we try, how long I dream of us
staying together, we are a broken record that continues to
skip, repeating the same song that is no longer beautiful.

11:53 P M

The words roll off your tongue so smoothly that I almost don't feel the pain.

Your voice has soothed me for so long that when you use that same voice to tell me we are over, I initially don't even register you are delivering bad news.

It's like you, the love of my life, are standing in front of me with your sweet and sympathetic eyes as if nothing is wrong and then you pull the trigger. So unexpected that I sit there, staring at my wound, misunderstanding the events that have just occurred.

"Why am I bleeding? How did this come to be? Did you really just say we—?

"Oh. I see."

My eyes rest on your mouth, the weapon that has fired against my heart.

11:59 PM

It takes hours to get to know someone, really get to know them, weeks to build a relationship and months to fall truly in love.

But all that could end up being for nothing because in one second your entire world could fall apart.

One second.

That's all it took for him to break my heart.

MIDNIGHT

You left me there wondering why, how,
what did I do wrong?

Gutted my love and let every last drop drain away.

Until all that was left of me was a heap of clattering bones.

12:01 A M

It was a wicked game you played with my heart.

Pulling on strings as though I were your puppet
and you the master.

12:08 AM

Over the years I had built a home for my heart. Four white walls with a ceiling of crafted glass that reflected the shapes and colors of the blue sky. Faith resided within.

I was a church.

The house of God.

You came into my life begging for forgiveness of your sins.

You left, setting it on fire.

12:22 A M

I tried loving you.

I tried really hard.

But you wanted more than I could give.

I was a broken soul abused by merciless boys
with bad intentions.

She had everything I lacked. An innocent and untouched
heart which you mistakenly thought was better.

Oh, by God, were you wrong.

I have had all this love festering inside waiting to be released
on the right person.

The person I know won't leave me so complicated and
broken.

She has never even come close to feeling the immense
devotion I have orbiting my soul.

She is only a star within my entire galaxy, but you looked at
her and thought she was the sun.

12:30 AM

You are the plaque on my heart. I try to brush you away but you hide in hard to reach places. You are a weakness, a cavity, an aching pain every time I breathe.

12:41 A M

My breath is rotten as your name spoils on my lips.

12:53 A M

I took the sweet parts of me and painted them on your rotten heart. I used my light to illuminate your dark parts. And when you didn't change, when you didn't bring your guard down, I gave you more. I poured and poured and poured all I had into your body, into your soul, until I had nothing left. My heart empty, my eyes tired, the light gone.

I lost myself while loving you.

1:16 AM

As I have grown

and loved

and been heartbroken,

I have learned that some fairy tales do not end with a
happily ever after.

Some end with an abrupt and bitter goodbye.

Period.

1:21 A M

You are the sand that doesn't stick when I am dry and sad.

1:26 A M

He is all I've ever wanted.

But he is not at all what I wanted.

The idea of him was appealing.

Addicting.

But he, himself, I didn't actually care for.

Which I guess makes me heartless.

And maybe I am.

Because I don't feel anything anymore.

That's why I wanted him in the first place.

To make me feel something again.

1:43 A M

You took the light parts of me and turned them dark.

2:01 AM

2 AM

you're still here

in my head

haunting me.

2:08 AM

We are all infected with false verifications of beauty.

They eat away at our hearts until the mirror is shattered and we soon forget who we are.

2:12 A M

My body is cold and my mind is numb. The absence of him is absolute zero.

The chill is in the goosebumps on my neck, once raised by the warmth of his lips. It is in the vacant spot in my bed where his head used to rest. It is in the constant ache in my heart, the pain that shears through. Making me bleed out-- not of blood, but of longing and wanting and regret.

2:22 A M

You grew out of me.

Shed me like snakeskin

and left me wrinkled on the floor.

2:28 A M

You are five thousand miles away.

I deleted your number.

There's no way to speak to you.

I have nothing to say.

I have no feelings for you anymore.

We are over.

But really . . .

You are ten miles away.

I have those digits memorized.

I could drive right over.

Knock on your door

and spill my heart out

onto your welcome mat.

We are nowhere close to over.

The distance between our bodies is small.

The distance between our hearts is infinite.

The distance between me still loving you, well,
there is no distance at all.

2:36 A M

How do I sleep when every time I close my eyes,
darkness engulfs my world?

The darkness you used to keep away.

2:55 AM

The monsters don't live in my closet or under my bed.

They are the collection of thoughts inside my head.

2:59 AM

I am broken because every time I hear that song or watch
that movie or read that book I think of you and
a piece of me falls away.

3:00 AM

I'm standing in the center of a crowded room

and I'm still only searching for your ghost.

3:01 AM

You are a connoisseur of the art of leaving

(me behind).

3:02 A M

There are three
words I roll
over and over
in my mouth.
They have a
terrible taste and
smell of heartache
but I can't
seem to spit
them out. They
just continue to
burn.

I miss you.

      I miss you.

            I miss you.

3:03 AM

I need my heart to be cleansed of your name, no matter how hard I must scrub, scrape, or scour it.

Yet somehow you managed to engrave each letter upon it where no amount of force can take it away.

And now, every beat, my heart echoes with the faint sound of your name.

3:09 A M

I have a hole in my heart waiting to be filled. I crave the taste of someone else's lips on mine and their heart intertwined with my soul.

3:11 AM

And so you're nineteen lying in your bedroom, eyes damp and breaths heavy, wondering why love hasn't swung your way. Although you know young love is just false hope, you still crave to be wanted by another heartbeat. Your name on someone else's lips and spoken softly in your ear. But there is this vast void between now and then that terrifies you deep down to your bones. Background noise becomes haunting thoughts. The idea that you won't ever be wanted. You won't find someone who will unconditionally love you. You might never feel reciprocated love. So you sit there in the shades of grey and pray that one day your thoughts will be proven wrong. Until then you dream endless fantasies of how it would be. You drape your arms over your ghost and dance the night away. You lie in bed and stare at the vacant spot next to you and whisper conversations you wish to have. Because it's the closest thing you have to what you so desperately want and even though it only blackens the void more, you're addicted to the feeling of being loved. If only it were real…

3:38 A M

I cannot find my heart.

I press my palm to my chest;

there is no beat,

no pulse,

nothing there at all.

It rests with you.

Transfused with the last kiss.

The goodbye.

It rests with you.

I am a living ghost.

No heart, no love, no one to hold.

3:40 A M

I believe we are destined for one person on this earth.

But the sad truth is, we do not always end up finding them.

3:46 A M

He will remain a star in the night sky.

I'll always try but I'll never reach him.

3:52 A M

I indulge myself in a book because diving headfirst into
another fantasy is so much more peaceful than
living in this reality.

3:59 AM

Absent lips,

vacant touch,

you were the one I loved so much.

Eyes that wander,

lips that kiss

all the women on your list.

I screamed and cried

until one day

I broke in half, forced you away.

You don't deserve me,

I know that now,

but I still crave your touch somehow.

4:36 A M

Days, months, years could pass before you call me on my cell phone.

And I will still be sitting here waiting for your ringtone.

4:38 A M

Here I am.

Here's who I want to be.

How do I get from point A to point B?

4:41 AM

I roll down the window while driving down 405 and put my hand out. It is immediately thrown back by the strength of the wind. But then I gain composure and push my hand forward and open it so that my palm faces the coming sunrise and my fingers are sprawled apart. There I can feel the wind run through them wildly

and I think of you

and your hair and your clothes and all of the other things my fingers used to run through.

4:43 A M

The stars seem stitched into the sky tonight.

My eyes are weaving in and out of their constellations.

These are the moments I have felt closest to the earth.

These are when I feel I have found myself.

You will, if not already, find yourself too.

And if you ever lose that, just look up at the stars.

Their light always leads the way.

4:44 A M

There were things I wanted to put on paper

but the words hurt too much to write.

4:49 A M

Sometimes emotions surge so strongly that words will never do them justice. So I sit here and stare at a blank page while storms brew inside me.

4:50 AM

You've got me writing again. Not sure if that's a good thing or a bad one. You've reopened my heart and my feelings spill onto the page. I write of adventures and crazy wonders and love. But as each memory is committed to paper, the ending draws near. I look down and find my paper dyed black from the hurt I've accidently poured.

4:57 AM

My heart is stained with the salty sadness I won't let taint my cheeks. As my eyes remain dry, my heart grows heavy. Each unshed tear falling to add to its weight. One day it will be so heavy that my body will no longer be able to hold it. It will plummet into a dark, empty void and the drumbeat of my existence will cease.

5:01 AM

How terribly tragic is it that someone's heart can be so shattered that they no longer even find the beauty in existing? That they'd rather endure the split-second pain of a bullet wound to release a lifetime of aching in their soul.

4:02 AM

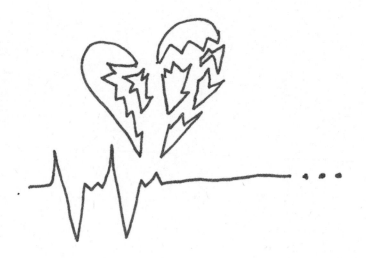

How did I make you feel?

I look back and think of all the things I could have done, should have said, but never did.

I see this boring and insecure version of myself when I was with you. And I see that person in the future too.

I can't imagine anyone loving me, being infatuated with my existence, if I couldn't even be that person to you.

5:16 A M

"Do you miss me?"

Every single day. I ache for you to hold me again. I can't fall asleep without a thought of you dragging me down. Our past makes a presence in all of my dreams and I continue to picture you in my future despite your abandonment.

"No."

5:17 AM

I'm so naive
to think
that a past lover
still loves me.
That one phone call
means I want you and
one hangout
means I miss you.
I'm stuck living in the past.
How do I get out of that
when I like those times better
than the lonely times today?
But I need to because it kills me
to relive each moment and memory,
thinking if this or that were changed,
you or I would have stayed.
Or if the timing was a little different
I'd be in your arms.
Even if the time was right,
Would you choose me and my broken heart?
If somehow I could manage the clocks
and go back to when we met,
I wouldn't change a single thing
except that I'd want you back.

5:18 AM

Love is a confusing thing and needs to be held with
gentle hands.

5:26 A M

When he talks about her

I can feel myself both smile and wince at the same time.

I am happy he is happy.

That's all I've ever wanted for him.

But I've always hoped he would find that happiness
with me.

5:28 A M

They cancel each other out, like us.

"Are you saying we cancel each other out?"

I'm saying you cancel me out.

When I was with you I felt like nothing. I didn't even feel like a whole person. I was just a body that you dragged along wherever you thought to wander.

We were supposed to add to each other. Build each other up and complement our differences.

But instead we were just two different operations that couldn't logically exist in the same equation.

5:30 A M

DAWN

Love is something absolutely beautiful. Yes, it may tear me apart and make me vulnerable as hell but it also is one of the only things in life worth living for.

Love allowed me to find someone who accepted me for my differences and embraced me for who I was. Someone to hold my hand when my world was falling apart and tell me "everything is going to be alright."

Yes, love killed me when I got left behind or forgotten, but I have to remember the times it ignited our hearts with fiery flames and allowed us to burn together.

5:32 A M

It's been five months.

I hadn't slept since.

But last night the rain returned and pounded on my window
and somehow my eyes managed to close. I did dream of
you, yes, but I slept.

I actually slept.

For the longest time I was puzzled as to why I only
found peace when it rained, but as I write this I'm beginning
to realize.

The raindrops that tap against my window rhythmically
mimic the drumbeat of your heart. The one I used to fall
asleep next to.

5:46 A M

It was so nice to hear your voice again.

And see that smile.

And feel the warmth of your body folding around me.

It was brief.

But it was nice.

5:49 A M

You left,

but you never really

left.

Does that make sense?

5:57 AM

Maybe it was all in my head. Maybe the way I saw things, felt things, was just me and you didn't think a thing of it.

Maybe our versions of reality are polar opposites and you never felt anything while I carried the weight of the world inside my heart.

6:00 AM

There will always be a rope between you and me. When we drifted apart years ago we never cut it— for we never said goodbye. We called it a "break." A pause to be resumed at a later time.

It's just that the break, the pause, didn't end and the rope that binds us together remains uncut.

You and I? We will always be connected. It may show up in a song or a place or in the depths of lonely nights. My name will always be at the back of your mind and yours will always have a place in my heart. So long as that rope remains between us.

6:13 A M

The history of us has already faded. There are few witnesses left able to recall. Yet it is still vivid in my mind.

The touch of you, the taste of you, the colors of your soul.

6:15 AM

You watered the flowers in my soul. You helped me grow into the person I am today.

I understand why you left. You came to teach me how to tend my own garden rather than helplessly wait for someone else to do so.

So although I wish you would have stayed, I am thankful that you didn't.

Only in your absence did I learn I can survive on my own just fine.

6:27 A M

You are a stranger now, but your eyes will always
be familiar.

6:33 AM

I cannot love you again.

You burned that bridge to the ground.

But years have gone by and you have changed.

I cannot love you again.

But I'd like to be a part of your life.

And you a part of mine.

Maybe we can rebuild that infrastructure and hold hands
not as lovers, but as friends.

6:34 A M

The morning sky seemed to melt into itself. The clouds cleared and bowed as the sun peeked over the horizon. Yellows and purples blended together creating lilac poetry within the sunrise. As I drove farther from your house, as I put more miles between us, I looked up and saw what God had painted for me.

That's when I knew that everything was going to be okay.

Definitely not today, probably not tomorrow, maybe not for a long while…

but eventually.

6:40 AM

If you are reading this,

I guess I just want you to know that you meant a lot to me.

Now? You've changed, I've changed.

You're a stranger.

I'm a memory.

I don't miss you anymore, I miss the idea of you.

But sometimes I get those two confused.

6:43 A M

Often we do not realize until it's too late.

We do not realize until the goodbye is stamped on our hearts.

We do not realize until it hurts.

Then we look back with heavy eyes and say,

"Oh, that must have been love."

7:00 A M

I will not apologize for things I shouldn't.

If someone demands those words and then walks out the door when I fail to deliver, I will let them.

They no longer have a place in my life.

They do not deserve me.

7:07 AM

I will no longer look for a man when I feel empty. I have learned this only postpones the heartache. They may come to me in my time of need and fill the holes in my heart, but they will soon grow tired of this chore, and leave me feeling emptier than before.

7:12 AM

Suddenly I woke up one morning and you weren't
my first thought.

I looked out the window and thought of what a good day
it was going to be rather than how broken I still am since
you left.

You were still there, in the back of my head.

But you were not first.

I'd call that progress.

7:43 A M

There has been a weight lifted off my shoulders.

To be so close to having love and then watching it fall away has brought me relief. Relief!

As soon as I told you goodbye I felt relieved, and that's how I know it was never right in the first place.

You should never watch love walk away and be content with that. If so, it was never love in the first place.

7:54 A M

It's the little things I miss.

The shape of your smile,

the glint in your ocean eyes,

and the way you pronounced each letter of my name.

8:04 AM

Let the music fill the empty patches of your soul.

And heal you.

8:36 A M

Self love is survival.

Without that, oxygen won't do a damn thing.

8:38 AM

I have decided today to love myself and look in the mirror
and smile.

Even though my first thought may be negative,
my actions will no longer be.

I am choosing

to love me

for me.

8:39 A M

How does it make you feel to know that although you led my heart into a state of great brokenness and fragility, you also led me to great success?

- You inspired these words
(and now the world gets
to read them)

8:42 AM

Pen and paper have healed me much better than any doctor ever could.

8:47 AM

If I look into a mirror and don't like what I see, I won't change my appearance.

I'll change my mindset.

9:15 AM

Eventually you will hit a crossroads and you will have four choices with no compass to guide you.

This may be the biggest decision of your life.

Please, whatever you do, do not turn around and walk back the way you came.

You didn't come this far only to give up when your path is no longer clear.

9:23 A M

To read poetry is such a gift.

To experience the works of

my brothers and sisters,

to soak in the lovely words,

awful words,

tragic words,

is like planting seeds inside me.

To write poetry is such a passion.

To bleed emotions onto a blank

page for others to embrace.

To create this delicate art,

fragile art,

beautiful art,

is like watering that garden

instilled in me ever since I could read,

and finally watching it grow.

9:30 AM

All in all, this book is not only about the love we hold for others. It is about self love.

You do not need a man to make you feel whole. You should feel that on your own.

And you need to understand that you must first love yourself before allowing another person to do so.

10:56 AM

There will come a point where everything falls into place. Everything makes sense. Why this didn't happen, why that did. Every past experience, moment, and memory is just that: in the past. And you won't look back. You'll be too busy living in the present world enjoying your beautiful life without hesitations or fear of anything. You'll catch yourself smiling for no apparent reason except the realization that this is your life and you are here for it.

It might seem absurd to you right now. It might not. Maybe the world is weighing down on you; you feel like you're drowning and there is no way to make it stop. No way to reach the light in whatever dark void you've found yourself. Maybe you haven't even found yourself at all.

Your time is coming.

I remember feeling empty, alone, scared of the world and what it had in store for me. I remember having these fears of judgement and failure and letting these drive my actions each day. I remember my late nights, the ones where I would spend hours sitting in darkness thinking "Is this how the rest of my life will be? What if it doesn't change?" Even worse: "What if I keep believing it will and then it never does?"

But it does. I can promise you that. People always say that, I know, but I've experienced this and once you do too you'll understand these words and the power they carry.

These bits and pieces of yourself that you own are soon to fall into place. And you will feel like you are on top of the world. Your entire outlook on life might even change.

How do I know?

Well, I'm sitting here writing this and smiling for no apparent reason except the realization that this is my life

and I'm here for it.

NOON

I am honored to be able to thank the following people:

James DeBono, who happened to stumble upon these words and, instead of pushing them to the side, believed in them, believed in me.

Michelle Halket and Central Avenue Publishing, who truly brought this project to life. You have made what I once thought an impossible dream of mine become a reality.

Abi, who saw a light in me and made sure not a single day went by that she didn't tell me so. I cannot thank you enough for your constant support, appreciation, and love.

Hailey, who from the minute I told her I wanted to write a book was on board and ready to dive headfirst on this journey. Boy, what a journey it has been. Thank you for having faith in my abilities, sticking by my side through all these years, and, of course, your beautiful illustrations.

Madison & Macie, who are always honest, caring, and know how to make me laugh even on days where that seems impossible. You both are my forever friends. I love you with everything I have.

Mom & Dad, who have raised me to be the woman I am. I would be nowhere without you. I love you to the moon and back (and then some).

You, who picked up these pages in some bookstore and decided to hold on to them for a while. You make all of this possible. You make dreams come true.

Makenzie Campbell grew up in the Pacific Northwest and has been expressing herself through poetry since grade school. *2am Thoughts* was something she kept to herself until she felt compelled to share it with the world and gathered enough confidence to do so. Makenzie is pursuing a degree in psychology at Washington State University, and her little free time is spent traveling and exploring the wild trails of the Cascades.

2am Thoughts is her first book.

@makenzie.campbell.poetry

WHAT WOULD YOU WRITE AT 4PM?

What are your 2am Thoughts?

And how do you feel when dawn breaks?

send your 2am thoughts to:

2amthoughtsbook@gmail.com